ENGINEERING FEATS

Three Gorges Dam

Earle Rice Jr.

Mitchell Lane

PUBLISHERS

2001 SW 31st Avenue
Hallandale, FL 33009
www.mitchelllane.com

627.8
Ric
E

Mitchell Lane
PUBLISHERS

Printing   1   2   3   4   5   6   7   8

Designer: Sharon Beck
Editor: Jim Whiting

Library of Congress Cataloging-in-Publication Data
Names: Rice, Earle, author.
Title: The Three Gorges Dam / by Earle Rice Jr.
Description: Hallandale, FL : Mitchell Lane Publishers, 2018. | Series: Engineering feats | Includes bibliographical references and index. | Audience: Grades 4 to 6.
Identifiers: LCCN 2017046704 | ISBN 9781680201727 (library bound)
Subjects: LCSH: San Xia Dam (China)—Juvenile literature.   11/18
Classification: LCC TC558.C52 S267 2018 | DDC 627/.80951212--dc23
LC record available at https://lccn.loc.gov/2017046704

eBook ISBN: 9-781-68020-173-4

CONTENTS

Words in **bold** throughout can be found in the Glossary.

1
Dragons, Dams, and Disasters

People live alongside great rivers because they are easy places to find food to eat and water to drink. They enable people to travel in boats and provide a convenient source of water to grow crops. But rivers are also prone to floods.

Chinese legend tells the story of a massive flood that washed over the land a long time ago. Waves taller than a 30-story building crashed into villages and demolished them. Heavy rains caused rivers to overflow. The Great Flood, as it became known, occurred about 2000 BCE (BEFORE COMMON ERA). It was actually a series of floods that lasted for decades. The floods began during the reign of Emperor Yao and continued through the reign of his successor Emperor Shun. The emperors called on Gun, a trusted official, to control the flood-waters. Gun built a series of dams and dikes. They didn't have any effect. The misery continued.

In desperation, Emperor Shun turned to Gun's son Yu. Yu was keenly aware of the problem. "The inundating waters seemed to assail the heavens, and in their extent embraced the hills and overtopped the great mounds, so that the people were bewildered and over-whelmed,"[1] he said. To deal with the issue, he tried a different method than his father. "I opened passages for the streams throughout the nine provinces and conducted them to the seas," he explained. "I deepened the channels and conducted them to the streams."[2]

Emperor Yao was regarded as one of the most morally correct and intelligent Chinese emperors. According to legend, his reign lasted for nearly a century. But he couldn't overcome the forces of nature. The artist is Ma Lin, whose career flourished during the early and middle parts of the 13th century—more than 2,000 years after Yao.

This statue in China of Emperor Shun, titled *Filial Piety Moves the Heavens*, honors the emperor's devotion to his widowed father. Shun respected his stepmother and loved his half brother even though they tried to kill him.

Such a massive task was clearly too much for a single man to accomplish. So, as the legend has it, Yu enlisted a team of dragons and set to work.

Yu and his dragons carved out new river beds to drain the floodwaters into the ocean. They altered the courses of some of the rivers to make them less likely to flood. Their work changed China's geography. One of the greatest changes was to move Yun Ling Mountain and place it in the Yangtze River. The mountain blocked the river's southward course and forced its waters to turn north. By means of this **mythical** movement, China's greatest river—called Chang Jiang, or "Long River"—remained flowing entirely in Chinese territory so its people could take advantage of its lifegiving water.

Yu controlled the floods and reshaped the face of China throughout a lifetime of service. He reaped great rewards for his work. Emperor Shun later chose him as his successor. What happened to Yu's team of dragons remains unclear. As emperor, Yu became known as Da Yu—the Great Yu. But despite Yu's lifelong struggle, the floods he controlled in his lifetime long outlasted him.[3]

In China, floods were—and still are—a way of life. They have claimed the lives of millions of people. A major flood occurs at least once every ten years. One of the worst floods in recent times occurred in 1954. During a long rainy season, with heavy rains in the middle reach of the Yangtze, the great river overflowed. The flooding claimed the lives of some 30,000 people. This tragic loss of life sparked renewed interest in building new dams for flood control on the Yangtze.

Such dams would regulate river levels and flooding downstream. They would help control flooding by storing the flood volume in **reservoirs** and releasing it later.

Flood control isn't the only reason to build dams. Even before the age of the Great Yu, dams served as ways of supplying water to **irrigate** crops.

The Great Yu, a legendary ruler in ancient China, gained fame for introducing flood control to his flood-ravaged nation (c.2000 BCE). Legend holds that he drained the Chinese empire of the waters of a mighty deluge using tortoise shells as drain pipes. Yu also used dragons to dredge riverbeds and develop a system of irrigation canals to channel floodwaters into the fields.

As the needs of developing civilizations increased, so did the uses for dams. They are now used not only for flood control, water supply, and irrigation, but also for navigation, **sedimentation** control, and hydropower.

To people living under the threat of losing their livelihoods, their homes, or even their lives to floods, flood control is of paramount importance among all these uses.

Nowhere is this more evident than on the long and mighty Yangtze. From its source high in the Tanggula Mountains near Tibet, it winds nearly 4,000 miles (6,500 meters) to the East China Sea. Close to 400 million people live in the regions along the Yangtze and its tributaries. The Yangtze River Basin covers one-fifth of China's total land area.[4] It forms the

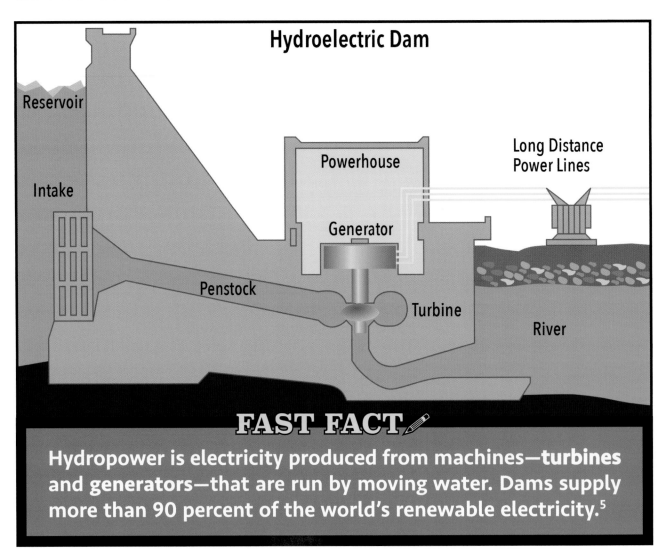

Hydroelectric Dam

Reservoir

Intake

Powerhouse

Long Distance Power Lines

Generator

Penstock

Turbine

River

FAST FACT

Hydropower is electricity produced from machines—**turbines** and **generators**—that are run by moving water. Dams supply more than 90 percent of the world's renewable electricity.[5]

"rice bowl" of China, producing 70 percent of the nation's staple food item.

In the late spring, melting mountain snows and **monsoon** rains raise the water level of the Yangtze. When its riverbanks can no longer contain its rising waters, more than one-third of a billion people and China's food supply are at risk. For thousands of years, the Chinese struggled and failed to contain the seasonal fury of the river they call Chang Jiang. At long last, they may have found a way to tame its wild waters and harness its boundless energy.

On the threshold of the 21st century, work commenced on the Three Gorges Dam. Supporters of the project said it would control flooding and supply electricity for millions of people. Critics call it a model for disaster. "With a project of this size there are bound to be some problems," writes Philip Wilkinson in his book *Yangtze*, "but it is hard to imagine that there will not be some benefits too."[6]

Qutang Gorge

Wu Gorge

Xiling Gorge

FAST FACT ✏

The Three Gorges lie between the cities of Fengjie and Yichang on the upper reaches of the Yangtze River. In descending order on the river, they are Qutang Gorge, Wu Gorge, and Xiling Gorge.

2

Dreaming Big

In China, Sun Yat-sen (1866–1925) is known as the "Father of the Nation." Sun became president of China in 1919. He had big dreams of modernizing China and fought hard to industrialize his country. To help accomplish this goal, he proposed building a big dam across the Yangtze River in his "Plan to Develop Industry"[1] in China soon after his presidency began.

He believed that a dam built downstream of the Three Gorges could generate 22 **gigawatts** of power. That is enough electricity to power 6.5 million homes! It would also help to control flooding. And its system of **ship locks** would enable large ships to voyage farther inland on the river. A ship lock provides a way of raising or lowering ships or other vessels between stretches of water at different levels on a river or canal. It is a fixed chamber in which the water level can be varied to raise or lower the ship like a water-borne elevator. If the water levels are significantly different, multiple locks must be used.

It was a big dream for a big project. But Sun Yat-sen was never known to dream small. More than 80 years later, Sun's dream finally came true: The Three Gorges Dam started up in 2003. It became fully operational in 2012.[2]

Like China's Long River, turning Sun Yat-sen's dream into reality followed a long and twisting course. Sun drew seven design concepts for his dream dam. Before he died in 1925, he passed them along to his successor, Chiang Kai-shek.

Sun Yat-sen, China's revered leader at the turn of the 20th century, posed serenely for this photograph in Canton in 1924. He dreamed of a great dam on the Yangtze River in 1919. Sun passed his dreams for modernizing China to Chiang Kai-shek (inset) in 1925.

Chiang also recognized that energy from the Yangtze River would be a key element in China's future development. Accordingly, he approved a survey on ways to improve the river's course. J. S. Lee, a Chinese **geologist**, conducted the initial survey in the 1930s. He suggested the best site might be where the river turned near the village of Sandouping (san-DOO-ping). George Barbour, Lee's American associate, agreed.[3] But the outbreak of war with Japan in July, 1937—and later World War II—put a stop to further planning.

A Chinese oarsman propels American Dr. John L. Savage and a Chinese delegation upriver on the Yangtze in a sampan in 1944.

In 1944, late in World War II, China's leaders began looking ahead to postwar development. They revived plans for a dam on the Yangtze. They needed help, and John Savage provided it. Savage was an American dam expert with the U.S. Bureau of Reclamation. He had worked on all the major dams of his time, such as the Hoover Dam on the Colorado River in Nevada and the Grand Coulee Dam on Washington state's Columbia River. Savage selected a site at the mouth of the Xiling Gorge near Nanjingguan (nan-JING-gwan). But in 1947, Chiang Kai-shek began to lose control of China to the **communist** forces of Mao Zedong. That brought all design work on the dam to a halt.

Mao's troops seized control of mainland China in 1949. Sun Yat-sen's dream now passed to Mao. As chairman of the Communist Party of China, Mao ruled the new People's Republic of China (PRC). In 1953, he proposed a dam at the Three Gorges. Following the tragic flooding along the Yangtze in 1954, Mao enlisted the aid of engineers from the Soviet Union the following year. They provided design and planning assistance.

All things connected with water—bridges, dams, and canals—fascinated Chairman Mao. He began to see them as symbols of victory over water. By extension, their development put his own power on display for China and the rest of the world to see. Mao further demonstrated his power by swimming across the Yangtze in the summer of 1956. It was about a mile wide at that point. Shortly afterward, he wrote the poem "Swimming" to mark the event. The second and last stanza looks at the challenges he faced:

This monument in Wuhan's Yanjiang Park, near the shore of the Yangtze River in Hankou, honors the people of Wuhan for overcoming the Yangtze Flood of 1954. The obelisk bears Mao Zedong's dedication inscription (top) and the text of his 1966 poem "Swimming" (bottom).

FAST FACT ✎

It took engineers and government officials 40 years just to choose the exact site for the Three Gorges Dam. And 35 more years passed from the time of Sun Yat-sen's proposal until work even began.

In this artist's rendering, the imposing figure of Chinese Chairman Mao Zedong towers over the riverine countryside at Wuhan. A mural (inset) marks the spot where Mao swam the Yangtze River in 1966.

Great plans are afoot:
A bridge will fly to span the North and
  South
Turning a barrier into a thoroughfare.
Walls of stone will stand upstream to the
  west
To hold back Wushan's [a geographical area
  in the Three Gorges] clouds and rain
Till a smooth lake rises in the narrow gorges.
The mountain Goddess, if she is still there,
Will marvel at a world so changed.[4]

Clearly, Mao foresaw a great dam at the gorges. He also recognized the great changes it would produce. He directed Zhou Enlai, the first premier of the PRC, to begin planning.

In May 1959, the Yangtze Valley Planning Office (YVPO) finally identified Sandouping as the site for the dam. Once again, however, China's internal affairs got in the way of the dam's development.

Mao had begun to feel that China's communist leaders were moving both the party and China itself in the wrong direction. He believed they were losing their commitment to the revolution. And he worried that he might be losing control of the government. To renew the revolutionary spirit and reassert his authority, in 1966 he launched what became known as the Cultural Revolution.

Chairman Mao called on China's urban youth to cleanse the nation of its corrupted elements. He urged a return to the ideals that had led his communist forces to victory nearly 20 years earlier. For the next 10 years, political and social upheaval prevailed in the country, as Mao struggled to regain his **dominance**. Work on the Three Gorges project ceased again.

3

Starts and Stops

During the Cultural Revolution, Mao practiced a different kind of communism than the Soviet Union. He believed the Soviets had departed from its pure form. Differences in how the beliefs of communism should be applied resulted in each country not trusting the other. Mao even began to worry that the Soviets would launch an attack on China. He rethought the timing of building a dam at the Three Gorges. He feared that the massive structure might become an easy military target. Mao put the project on hold again. Nevertheless, in 1970 he supported the idea of a smaller dam on the Yangtze called the Gezhouba Dam. It would be located near Yichang City in Hubei Province.

Mao told his planners that he was concerned about flooding. He wondered what would happen if the dam were to be bombed and destroyed. They informed him that the amount of water released by the smaller dam would not cause a "serious disaster." Mao gave in. "I approve construction of the Gezhouba Dam," he said. But he warned, "What is proposed in the documents is one thing, unexpected problems and difficulties that will arise during construction are another. Therefore, you must be ready to revise the design of the project."[1] His words proved true.

Workers broke ground for the Gezhouba Dam on December 30, 1970. In 1972, countless design changes forced a work stoppage. The dam was completely redesigned. Work resumed in October 1974,

A lock at the Gezhouba Dam closes behind riverboats before filling with water to lift them to a higher level. The dam (inset) rises above the Yangtze River at Yichang, Hubei Province, China.

FAST FACT ✎

The Gezhouba Dam was named for Gezhouba Island, one of two islands at the construction site. It was the first water conservancy project on the Yangtze River.[2]

under the supervision of Lin Yishan. Lin was a former party secretary and director of the Yangtze Valley Planning Commission. More than 100,000 laborers and soldiers worked on the dam.

The Gezhouba Dam was completed in December 1988, eighteen years after work began. Compared to most dams of that time, it was huge.

Gezhouba Dam, on the Yangtze River, viewed through hazy conditions at Yichang, China.

It measures 8,550 feet (2,606 meters) across and 177 feet (54 meters) high. Its reservoir contains 56 billion cubic feet (about 1.6 billion cubic meters) of water. At start-up, the dam generated 15 billion **kilowatts** of electricity a year, with more to come. And its three enormous locks are engineering marvels in their own right. They easily lift 10,000-ton ships from one level to another.[3] The cargo-carrying capacity of those ships turned the once-small town of Yichang into a bustling industrial city.

The many design and construction setbacks on the Gezhouba Dam served as a valuable learning experience for the Three Gorges project that would follow. Its location at the lower end of the Three Gorges would later help to regulate the tail water flow from the larger dam upstream. (Tail water is water below a dam.) This improves navigation. In time, the two dams would complement each other and operate "in sync."

Two views of the Gezhouba colossus on the Yangtze at Yichang, China.

Meanwhile, Chairman Mao Zedong died in 1976. His Cultural Revolution ended shortly after his passing. But planning for the Three Gorges Dam restarted. In 1984, China's ministry in charge of water and power recommended that construction begin. Workers built roads, harbors, and power plants near the Sandouping site. This site offered a solid rock foundation for the dam. Planners projected the dam's height as 491 feet (170 meters).

FAST FACT ✏

The Yangtze carries more than 500 million tons of silt—sand, clay, or other material—a year into the Three Gorges reservoir.[4] It drops to river bottoms and becomes sediment, which causes soil erosion.

Constructed during the Ming Dynasty, the Shibaozhai (Precious Stone Fortress) graced the banks of the Yangtze River for some 300 years in Zhongxian County, Chongqing Municipality, China. The fortress disappeared from view when the rising waters of the Three Gorges Reservoir reached the 512-foot (156-meter) mark in October 2006.

Not everyone saw the need for another expensive dam on the Yangtze. Critics thought the money might be better spent on education and health care. The National People's Congress put further planning on hold until 1987.

In the meantime, some engineers voiced concerns over the dam's proposed height. They thought it might cause major sedimentation problems for large cities like Chongqing (CHOONG-ching). Planners raised the height a little. Supporters thought that the added height would lessen the sediment problem. Lessening sediment would help reduce soil **erosion**.

A Canadian study completed in 1988 recommended construction at "an early date."[5] Both the Canadian and U.S. governments supported

Smog and the polluted waters of the Yangtze River at Chongqing Municipality, China, offer mute testimony to humankind's struggle to coexist with nature.

going ahead with a 607-foot (185 meters) version of the dam. It looked like the dam was about to be built. But a vote by the Chinese government was delayed. Continuing disagreements stalled the planning.

Two years later, Premier Li Peng directed a new group to review the program. In August 1991, the group endorsed the 607-foot dam. Though the U.S. Bureau of Reclamation had originally suggested such a dam, it later withdrew its support. It stated that "It is generally known that large-scale water retention projects are not environmentally or economically feasible."[6]

Despite continuing opposition to the dam, two key Chinese government agencies approved the dam in early 1992. The following April, the National People's Congress authorized a resolution to proceed with its construction. The vote was 1,767 for and 177 against. Some 664 members withheld their vote. The voting showed that opposition remained strong. Nevertheless, construction of the Three Gorges Dam finally started in mid-1994.

4

A Great Dam Rises

The Three Gorges Dam consists of a **gravity dam** with a **spillway** in the middle. (A spillway is a structure that controls the release of water from a dam.) Gravity dams are constructed of concrete or stone masonry. They hold back water primarily by their weight alone. A power house and a non-overflow section are located at both ends of the dam. Thirty-two main generators and two power generators convert the waters of the Yangtze to electricity.

The great dam measures 7,661 feet (2,310 meters) across, 377 feet (115 meters) in width, and stands 607 feet (185 meters) above sea level. Put another way, it is almost a mile and a half across, as wide as a football field is long, and stands as tall as a 60-story skyscraper. It was built by the state-backed China Yangtze Three Gorges Dam Project Development Corporation. More than 40,000 workers helped to build it.

The actual construction of the dam was completed a year early in 2008. From groundbreaking in 1994 to full operation in 2012, the entire project took 17 years. The Chinese government covered most of the dam's cost. Companies and banks from Canada, France, Germany, Switzerland, Sweden, and Brazil also contributed funds.

It was completed in three stages. Stage 1 (1993–1997) consisted of preparation work. To provide access to the dam site, workers cut a 17-mile road through the mountains of Xiling Gorge to Yichang at a

Three Gorges Dam

Gezhouba Dam

Diversion channel

May 2006

China's Three Gorges Dam

The world's largest hydroelectric project.

500 km
500 miles

CHINA

Beijing ★

Shanghai

Map area

Yangtze River

- More than 1 million people have been resettled
- About 12 cities, 140 towns, 1,300 villages will be submerged
- Lake behind dam will be 410 mi. (660 km) long

Yunyang • Fengjie • Wushan • *Xiling Gorge*

Wanxian • *Qutang Gorge* *Wuxia Gorge* • Yichang

Yangtze River

Zhongxian • **Three Gorges Dam**

Changshou • Fengdu

• Fuling

Chongqing

Yangtze River

Dam

River's flow

Dam's dimensions
- **Length**
  1.4 mi. (2.3 km), the world's longest
- **Height**
  606 ft. (185 m)

Energy production
85 billion kilowatt hours a year by 2009

Environmental impact

| **Threatened species:** Include Yangtze dolphin, Chinese sturgeon, finless porpoise | **Landmarks:** Scenic deep gorges, about 1,000 archaeological sites submerged | **Farmland:** About 60,500 acres (24,500 ha) of farmland, orchards flooded |

A view from space of the Yangtze River shows the Three Gorges Dam under construction and partially completed in July 2000, with an arrow directed toward a temporary diversion channel. This channel on the south bank allowed the river's sediment-filled water to continue flowing freely during the dam's construction. Temporary ship locks (bottom inset) for continuing vessel passage can be seen along the river's north bank in May 2006. The relative proximity of the Three Gorges Dam and the Gezhouba Dam (upper inset) as seen from space.

cost of $110 million.[1] The road included seven miles of bridges and tunnels.

Before work could begin on the dam itself, workers had to first create a **diversion channel**. This channel temporarily redirected the course of the river and let it continue to flow freely.

FAST FACT 🖉

Original estimates placed the cost of building the dam at $22.5 billion. The final figure was $59 billion.[2]

This was done by placing a series of stone **cofferdams** to block off sections of the river until the first sections of the dam were completed. They would later be replaced by concrete cofferdams. Cofferdams are large watertight chambers used for construction under water. The chambers are pumped dry to create a dry pit for laborers to work. Cofferdams are destroyed when they are no longer needed.

Stage 1 also included the construction of a temporary ship lock on the north bank of the river. The temporary lock ensured a smooth flow of shipping during construction.

The stage was completed in November 1997. In a speech to honor the occasion, China's President Jiang Zemin said, "It . . . embodies the great industrious and dauntless spirit of the Chinese nation and displays the daring vision of the Chinese people for new horizons and a better future in the course of their reform and opening up."[3]

Stage 2 (1998–2003) involved the construction of cofferdams both upstream and downstream of the dam. During this phase, the river water flowed through the diversion channel. Shipping used either the channel or the temporary ship lock. Permanent navigation buildings were completed on the north bank. Then the diversion channel was blocked, and the dam began storing water. As the walls of the dam rose, the water

Cofferdams are used to temporarily block off sections of a river while a dam undergoes construction. This cofferdam was located 374 feet (114 meters) upstream of the Three Gorges Dam. It stood about 459 feet (140 meters) high and measured some 1,902 feet (580 meters) in length. Workers reportedly positioned a total of 192 tons of dynamite in more than 1,700 locations for its eventual destruction. The cofferdam (inset) was demolished in June 2006.

Steel bars reinforced great slabs of concrete of the Three Gorges Dam under construction.

Two giant cranes standing amid a ship lock attest to the enormity of the lock under construction at the Three Gorges Dam in September 2001. A series of ship locks fill with water and raise or lower river vessels more than 300 feet (90 meters). A section of the Three Gorges Dam (inset) under construction in June 2003.

FAST FACT ✎

The Yangtze is the third-longest river in the world. Its length is exceeded by only the Nile River in Africa and the Amazon River in South America.

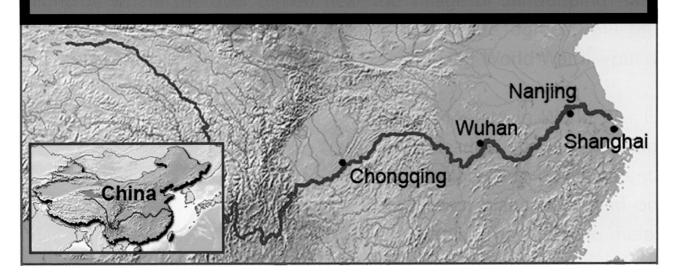

level rose behind them it at a rate of 13–16 feet (4–5 meters) a day.[4] Cracks appeared in the wall, and a lot of additional money was spent to repair them.

Stage 2 also saw the completion of a 443-feet (135 meter) permanent ship lock on the north bank. The system contains five chambers and is the largest of its kind in the world. It features two sets of staircase locks. One moves upstream, the other downstream. Because of the dam's construction, vessels must be lifted or lowered more than 300 feet (90 meters). Each of the five locks raises or lowers a vessel about 65 feet (20 meters).

During Stage 3 (2003–2009), 12 sets of main power generators were installed on the south bank in 2006 and another 14 sets on the north bank two years later. They became operational in October 2008 and generated a total of 18,000 megawatts of electricity. Six additional generators installed later brought the electricity production to 22,500 megawatts.

The Three Gorges Dam in an early stage of construction. A concept (inset) of the completed dam and ship locks.

When the great dam reached its full height, the water level rose to 574 feet (175 meters) above sea level. It formed a reservoir 410 miles (660 kilometers) long. That is longer than the state of Colorado! It is 3,675 feet (1.12 kilometers) wide. Its total surface area covers 403 square miles (1,045 km^2). The reservoir flooded a total area of 244 square miles (632 km^2) and contains 31.9 million-acre feet (39.3 km^3) of water.

A panoramic view of the ship locks and distant cantilever bridge at the Three Gorges Dam. An interior view (inset) of ships navigating through the locks.

Water gushes down the spillway of the Three Gorges Dam. Workers (left insert) install an electromotor commutator at the dam's hydroelectric power plant. Runner of a Francis turbine (right insert). The force of the river water striking the runner's specially designed blades causes the shaft of the turbine to rotate and generate power.

A Chinese author recently wrote of the Three Gorges Dam, "The project will not only make a contribution to the present but will also benefit the nation and people for centuries to come. The future of the Three Gorges will be more beautiful than ever."[5] But there is another side to the story of the greatest dam ever built.

5

The Good and the Bad

Based on how much electricity it generates, the Three Gorges Dam is the world's largest hydroelectric dam. It is truly a marvel of engineering. China can be—and is—proud of its remarkable achievement. From its inception in 1919 in the mind of Sun Yat-sen to its full operation in 2012, however, the dam has invited debate. Legions of supporters sing its praises. Opposing armies of critics complain of its ills. Arguments in favor of and against it continue.

Supporters quickly point to its ability to control flooding. By lowering the water level in its reservoir in controlled releases, it can make room for excess water during snow melts and heavy rains. Those stored waters can reduce flooding downstream and save countless lives. They also provide fresh water and **drought** relief in times of water scarcity. Power generated through the dam's 32 turbines now supplies electricity to millions of people for the first time. More hydropower helps reduce the use of coal to generate electricity and lessens the region's carbon footprint. Though the dam stands on two major fault lines, it is built to withstand a magnitude 7.0 earthquake.

Higher water levels also allow larger vessels to travel farther upriver. Increased shipping brings more business inland, turns villages into towns and towns into cities, and helps tourism grow. New roads and railways are built to accommodate new businesses. The economy flourishes.

In addition to the ship locks at Three Gorges Dam, a shiplift was incorporated into the dam's design to speed river traffic along the Yangtze. It is essentially an elevator for ships, capable of lifting ships up to 3,000 tons, using a helical gear system to climb or descend on a toothed rack. The shiplift, shown here lifting a boatload of tourists, became operational in September 2016. The inset views the shiplift from the outside.

At the same time, China is working to reduce the ecological impact of the dam. According to a government report, "China has invested tens of billions of **yuan** over the past decade in reducing soil erosion and building tree belts along the upper and middle reaches of the Yangtze."[2] To reduce pollution in the river, the city of Chongqing has installed four wastewater interceptors and two large-scale wastewater treatment plants. They have improved the appearance of the river and reduced floating debris. Further, a new landfill absorbs between 1,500 and 2,000 tons of waste a day.[3]

> ## FAST FACT ✎
>
> Planners originally estimated that electricity produced by the Three Gorges Dam would provide up to 10 percent of the nation's energy needs. During the dam's long construction period, China's increasing power needs reduced that estimate to about 3 percent.[1]

Critics of the Three Gorges Dam strongly condemn the human misery it caused by uprooting people from their homes, jobs, businesses, and farms. As the water level rose to fill the reservoir, 13 cities, 140 towns, and 1,350 villages became submerged. Over the course of the dam's construction, almost 1.3 million people were forced to move to make room for the dam and its expanding reservoir.[4] Many people lost their jobs. Farmers were moved from rich lands in the Yangtze Basin to less fertile lands elsewhere.

Corruption ran rampant. Officials stole an estimated 12 percent of funds set aside by the government to move people. One displaced person complained, "Our lives have been ruined by the dam while the big officials got their fruit and filled their wallet."[5]

The movement of so many people severely damaged the land. Forests were destroyed for wood to build new homes and improve navigation on the river. Soil eroded without tree roots to hold it firm. Landslides demolished cities and killed many people. Pollution control is not working well, say critics of the dam. And the possibility of a massive earthquake remains a threat to everyone in the region.

Treasured cultural **artifacts** were lost forever. Experts say that some 1,300 important cultural sites disappeared under the dam's rising waters.

FAST FACT

Displaced homeowners received a modest fee from the government for their houses. In many cases, the money did not cover the cost of another home at their new location.

A sign of things to come. In May 2006, a line on this billboard marked the projected water level—156 meters (512 feet)—of the Three Gorges Dam Reservoir at a soon-to-be-demolished business street at the port of Wushan. The city lies about 75 miles (120 kilometers) upstream of the dam. All of the port's wharf facilities eventually slipped beneath the reservoir's rising waters.

Among the most famous are the remnants of homeland sites of the ancient Ba people who once lived in the area. They are now lost for future generations to study.

Many archaeological artifacts and sites, as well as countless homes, surrendered their existence to the rising waters of the Three Gorges Dam reservoir. Workers labor here at the soon-to-be-submerged Tuanjie Village of Shituo Township in Fuling District of Chongqing Municipality. They are excavating an ancient city site covering an area of some 120,000 square yards (100,000 square meters). The site reportedly prospered during the Song Dynasty (960–1279).

Equally distressing to many is the dam's impact on the **ecology**. The dam has endangered many wildlife species and driven some to extinction. The endangered animals include the Chinese sturgeon, Chinese tiger, Chinese alligator, Siberian crane, and the giant panda. Environmental changes driven by the dam also threaten the existence of 6,400 plant species, 3,400 insect species, 300 fish species, and more than 500 land animals.[6]

Changes in the water also affect the animal and plant life downstream. Buildup of sediment in the reservoir has altered or destroyed spawning and breeding grounds in the floodplains, river deltas, beaches, and elsewhere. Chemical toxins released into the river by factories and other sources add to the pollution of their watery environment.

The camera captured this morass of floating garbage on the upper reaches of the Yangtze River, near the Three Gorges Dam in July 2013. Seasonal flooding creates large buildups of garbage on the river each year. Fisherman often double as garbage collectors to clear the wastes and supplement their incomes.

The respective cases for and against the Three Gorges Dam will likely continue for decades. Tang Changsi, a resident of the Yangtze Basin, recently praised the dam. "I keep on living a normal life when flood season comes every year," he said. "Without the dam, I would most likely be on the riverbanks fighting the flood right now."[7]

Dai Qing, a writer and strong critic of the dam, viewed the dam through different eyes. "If the Three Gorges could speak, they would plead for mercy."[8]

And so flows China's Long River—partly contained by the rise of a great dam, and awaiting the verdict of history.

WHAT YOU SHOULD KNOW

★ The Three Gorges Dam project was fully completed on July 4, 2012.

★ The dam consists of three main areas: the dam structure itself, a hydroelectric section, and a system of ship locks.

★ Construction of the dam occurred in three phases over a 17-year time frame.

★ Flood control, power generation, and improved navigation were the three main reasons for building the dam on the Yangtze River.

★ The physical dam was mostly completed in 2006.

★ Chinese author Dai Qing was imprisoned for writing a collection of essays critical of the dam. She estimates the final cost of the dam may exceed $88 billion.

★ Funding for the dam was denied by the World Bank due to environmental concerns.

★ Some of the best farming land in the Yangtze River Basin was flooded by the creation of the dam's reservoir.

★ It takes two-and-a-half hours to raise or lower large vessels more than 300 feet (90 meters) through the lock system. Smaller vessels are raised in about 40 minutes using an elevator-type lock.

★ About 150 freight-carrying ships pass through the lock system daily.

★ Work on the dam was conducted in three shifts, 24 hours a day, using 25,000 construction workers. Forty percent of the workers were women.

★ China plans to build over 100 more dams all across its southwest region.

QUICK STATS

★ The Three Gorges Dam is the world's largest power station in terms of its installed electrical capacity of 22,500 MW.

★ Energy produced by the dam equals the energy production of 15 nuclear power plants.

★ Construction of the dam increased shipping on the Yangtze River from 10 to 100 million tons annually.

★ The Three Gorges Dam is five times larger than the Hoover Dam in the United States.

★ Construction materials for the dam included 10.82 million tons of cement, 1.92 million tons of rolled steel, and 1.6 million cubic meters of wood.

★ Electricity produced by the dam replaces an estimated 50 million tons of coal. Clean electricity helps to reduce China's carbon footprint, emissions of greenhouse gases, and acid rain.

★ More than 80,000 sticks of dynamite were used during the first year of construction.

★ Over 100 workers were killed during the dam's long construction period.

★ The presence of the dam protects an estimated 15 million people and 1.5 million acres of farmlands from devastating floods.

★ China boasts the world's largest number of dams—86,000 and counting.

★ The 100,000 acres flooded in the Yangtze River Basin to create the dam's reservoir accounted for 10 percent of China's grain supply, 50 percent of which is rice.

1919	Chinese leader Sun Yat-sen proposes a dam at the Three Gorges on the Yangtze River.
1925	Sun Yat-sen dies; planning for the dam passes to Chiang Kai-shek.
1937	Outbreak of war with Japan interrupts planning on the dam.
1944	Chinese leaders revive plans for the dam.
1947	Officials stop all design work on the dam.
1953	Communist leader Mao Zedong proposes a dam at the Three Gorges.
1954	A major flood in the Yangtze River Basin claims the lives of 30,000 people. Mao enlists the aid of the Soviets on the dam.
1956	Mao Zedong swims across the Yangtze River.
1959	The Yangtze Valley Planning Office identifies Sandouping as the site for the dam.
1966	Mao launches the Cultural Revolution; planning for the dam is delayed.
1970	Work begins on the Gezhouba Dam.
1972	Design changes force a work stoppage on the Gezhouba Dam.
1974	Work resumes on the Gezhouba Dam.
1976	Mao Zedong dies and the Cultural Revolution ends.
1984	A Chinese ministry recommends the start of construction on the Three Gorges Dam.
1985	Planning for the Three Gorges Dam is put on hold until 1987.
1988	The Gezhouba Dam is completed. A Canadian study recommends the start of construction on the Three Gorges Dam.
1990	Premier Li Peng directs a new group to review the Three Gorges program; the group endorses a 607-foot-high dam in 1991.
1992	The National People's Congress authorizes a resolution to proceed with the dam's construction.
1994	Construction of the Three Gorges Dam commences.
2003	The Three Gorges Dam starts up.
2012	The Three Gorges Dam becomes fully operational.

CHAPTER NOTES

Chapter 1—Dragons, Dams, and Disasters

1. Xia Dynasty (2200-1700 B.C.): China's First Emperors, The Great Flood, and Evidence of Their Existence. Facts and Details.com. http://factsanddetails.com/china/cat2/sub1/entry-4278.html

2. Ibid.

3. Philip Wilkinson, *Yangtze* (London: BBC Books, 2005), pp. 36–37.

4. "Yangtze River Basin." My Yangtze Cruise. http://www.myyangtzecruise.com/yangtze-river-basin_12635_c/

5. "Role of Dams." International Commission on Large Dams. http://www.icold-cigb.org/GB/Dams/role_of_dams.asp

6. Wilkinson, *Yangtze*, p. 90.

Chapter 2—Dreaming Big

1. Peter H. Gleick, "Three Gorges Dam Project, Yangtze River, China." Water Brief 3. *The World's Water*, p. 147. http://worldwater.org/wp-content/uploads/2013/07/WB03.pdf

2. "China's Three Gorges Dam reaches operating peak." BBC. July 5, 2012. http://www.bbc.com/news/world-asia-china-18718406

3. Simon Winchester, *The River at the Center of the World: A Journey Up the Yangtze, and Back in Chinese Time* (New York: Henry Holt and Company, 1996), p. 221.

4. Ibid., p. 210.

5. "Cultural Revolution." History.com, 2009. http://www.history.com/topics/cultural-revolution

Chapter 3—Starts and Stops

1. Deirdre Chetham, *Before the Deluge: The Vanishing World of the Yangtze's Three Gorges* (New York: Palgrave Macmillan, 2002), p. 161.

2. "Gezhou Dam." Visit Our China. http://www.visitourchina.com/yichang/attraction/gezhou-dam.html

3. Philip Wilkinson, Yangtze (London: BBC Books, 2005), p. 101.

4. "Three Gorges Dam: A Model of the Past." International Rivers. https://www.internationalrivers.org/resources/three-gorges-dam-a-model-of-the-past-3512

5. Peter H. Gleick, "Three Gorges Dam Project, Yangtze River, China." Water Brief 3. *The World's Water*, p. 147. http://worldwater.org/wp-content/uploads/2013/07/WB03.pdf

6. Chetham, *Before the Deluge*, p. 167.

Chapter 4—A Great Dam Rises

1. Deirdre Chetham, *Before the Deluge: The Vanishing World of the Yangtze's Three Gorges* (New York: Palgrave Macmillan, 2002), p. 177.

2. Ping Zhou, "The Three Gorges Dam: The Three Gorges Dam is the World's Largest Hydroelectric Dam." ThoughtCo. March 3, 2017. https://www.thoughtco.com/three-gorges-dam-1434411

3. Chetham, *Before the Deluge*, p. 178.

4. "Water levels rise in Three Gorges dam, cracks appear." SMH.com.au. June 2, 2003. http://www.smh.com.au/articles/2003/06/01/1054406074110.html

5. Chetham, *Before the Deluge*, p. 219.

Chapter 5—The Good and the Bad

1. Brian Handwerk, "China's Three Gorges Dam, by the Numbers." *National Geographic News*, June 9, 2006. http://news.nationalgeographic.com/news/2006/06/060609-gorges-dam_2.html

2. "Yangtze." World Wildlife Fund. https://www.worldwildlife.org/places/yangtze

3. "Wastewater Treatment and Landfill Ease Pollution of China's Yangtze River." World Bank. December 13, 2007. http://www.worldbank.org/en/news/feature/2007/12/13/wastewater-treatment-landfill-ease-pollution-chinas-yangtze-river

4. "Three Gorges Dam: A Model of the Past." International Rivers. https://www.internationalrivers.org/resources/three-gorges-dam-a-model-of-the-past-3512

5. Ibid.

6. Ping Zhou, "The Three Gorges Dam: The Three Gorges Dam is the World's Largest Hydroelectric Dam." ThoughtCo. March 3, 2017. https://www.thoughtco.com/three-gorges-dam-1434411

7. Jin Zhu, "Residents of flood control region praise Three Gorges." *China Daily Asia*, July 16, 2012. http://www.chinadailyasia.com/news/2012-07/16/content_115289.html

8. Richard Perry Hayman, *Three Gorges of the Yangtze: Grand Canyons of China* (New York: Odyssey Publications, 2000), n.pag.

Currie, Stephen. *What Is the Future of Hydropower? The Future of Renewable Energy*. San Diego, CA: Reference Point Press, 2012.

Kite, L. Patricia. *Building the Three Gorges Dam*. North Mankato, MN: Heinemann-Raintree, 2011.

Mann, Elizabeth. *Hoover Dam. Wonders of the World*. Richmond Hill, Ontario, Canada: Miyaka Press, 2006.

Rice, Earle Jr. *The Yangtze River. Rivers of the World*. Hockessin, DE: Mitchell Lane Publishers, 2013.

Spilsbury, Louise. *Dams and Hydropower*. New York: Rosen Publishing Group, 2011.

WORKS CONSULTED

Barter, James. *The Yangtze. Rivers of the World*. Farmington Hills, MI: Lucent Books, 2003.

Chetham, Deirdre. *Before the Deluge: The Vanishing World of the Yangtze's Three Gorges*. New York: Palgrave Macmillan, 2002.

"China's Three Gorges Dam reaches operating peak." BBC. July 5, 2012. http://www.bbc.com/news/world-asia-china-18718406

"Cultural Revolution." History.com, 2009. http://www.history.com/topics/cultural-revolution

"Gezhou Dam." Visit Our China. http://www.visitourchina.com/yichang/attraction/gezhou-dam.html

Gleick, Peter H. "Three Gorges Dam Project, Yangtze River, China." Water Brief 3. *The World's Water*, 2008–2009. http://worldwater.org/wp-content/uploads/2013/07/WB03.pdf

Handwerk, Brian. "China's Three Gorges Dam, by the Numbers." *National Geographic News*, June 9, 2006. http://news.nationalgeographic.com/news/2006/06/060609-gorges-dam_2.html

Hayman, Richard Perry. *Three Gorges of the Yangtze: Grand Canyons of China*. New York: Odyssey Publications, 2000.

Jin Zhu. "Residents of flood control region praise Three Gorges." *China Daily Asia*, July 16, 2012. http://www.chinadailyasia.com/news/2012-07/16/content_115289.html

Ping Zhou. "The Three Gorges Dam: The Three Gorges Dam is the World's Largest Hydroelectric Dam." ThoughtCo. March 3, 2017. https://www.thoughtco.com/three-gorges-dam-1434411

"Role of Dams." International Commission on Large Dams. http://www.icold-cigb.org/GB/Dams/role_of_dams.asp

"Three Gorges Dam: A Model of the Past." International Rivers. https://www.internationalrivers.org/resources/three-gorges-dam-a-model-of-the-past-3512

"Wastewater Treatment and Landfill Ease Pollution of China's Yangtze River." World Bank. December 13, 2007. http://www.worldbank.org/en/news/feature/2007/12/13/wastewater-treatment-landfill-ease-pollution-chinas-yangtze-river

"Water levels rise in Three Gorges dam, cracks appear." SMH.com.au. June 2, 2003. http://www.smh.com.au/articles/2003/06/01/1054406074110.html

Wilkinson, Philip. *Yangtze*. London, UK: BBC Books, 2005.

Winchester, Simon. *The River at the Center of the World: A Journey Up the Yangtze, and Back in Chinese Time*. New York: Henry Holt and Company, 1996.

Wong, How Man. *Exploring the Yangtze: China's Longest River*. San Francisco: China Books & Periodicals, 1989.

Xia Dynasty (2200-1700 B.C.): China's First Emperors, The Great Flood, and Evidence of Their Existence. Facts and Details.com http://factsanddetails.com/china/cat2/sub1/entry-4278.html

"Yangtze River Basin." My Yangtze Cruise. http://www.myyangtzecruise.com/yangtze-river-basin_12635_c/

"Yangtze." World Wildlife Fund. https://www.worldwildlife.org/places/yangtze

ON THE INTERNET

Three Gorges Dam
http://www.academickids.com/encyclopedia/index.php/Three_Gorges_Dam

Three Gorges Dam
http://kids.britannica.com/comptons/art-123325/The-Three-Gorges-Dam-spans-the-Yangtze-River-near-Yichang

Three Gorges Dam
http://encyclopedia.kids.net.au/page/th/Three_Gorges_Dam

artifact (AHR-tih-fakt)—an object created by humans

cofferdam (KAH-fur-dam)—a large watertight chamber used for construction under water

conservancy (kon-SIR-vant-see)—an area used to conserve and protect natural resources

communist (KOM-yew-nist)—a party or supporter of a social system in which property is owned by the community and each member works for the common good

diversion channel (duh-VUHR-zhun CHAN-nuhl)—a temporary pathway where water is redirected

dominance (DOM-uh-nance)—commanding influence over a person or thing

drought (DROWT)—continuous dry weather without any rainfall

ecology (ee-KOL-uh-jee)—the scientific study of living things in relation to their environment

erosion (ih-ROH-zhun)—wearing away by the action of wind, water, or glacial ice

generator (JEN-eh-ray-tohr)—a machine for converting mechanical energy into electricity; in a dam, a turbine driven by the flow of water

geologist (jee-OL-a-jist)—an expert in the study of the Earth's crust and strata

gigawatt (JIH-guh-wot)—a unit of power equal to one billion watts

gravity dam—a concrete or stone masonry dam designed to hold back water by its weight alone

irrigation (ir-uh-GAY-zhun)— supplying land or crops with water by means of streams, channels, pipes, and so on

kilowatt (KIL-uh-wot)—the power of 1,000 watts

monsoon (mon-SOON)—of a seasonal wind in southeast Asia; rainy season

mythical (MITH-uh-kal)—existing in myth; imaginary, fancied

reservoir (REZ-er-vwahr)—a natural or artificial lake that is a source of water

sedimentation (sed-uh-men-TAY-shun)—process in which solid material such as sand and gravel is carried by wind or water and settles on the surface of land

ship lock—a device for raising or lowering ships or other water craft between stretches of water at different levels on a river or canal

spillway (SPILL-way)—a structure that controls the release of water from a dam

turbine (TUHR-bine)—a machine or wheel turned by the pressure of air, steam, water, or gas

yuan (yoo-AHN)—the basic monetary unit of the People's Republic of China; about seven yuan equals one U.S. dollar

ABOUT THE AUTHOR

Earle Rice Jr. is a former senior design engineer and technical writer in the aerospace, electronic-defense, and nuclear industries. He has devoted full time to his writing since 1993, and has written several books about China and the Far East. Earle is the author of more than ninety published books. He is listed in *Who's Who in America* and is a member of the Society of Children's Book Writers and Illustrators, the League of World War I Aviation Historians, the Air Force Association, and the Disabled American Veterans.